Red Lorry, Yellow Lorry

Fiona Waters is one of the most prolific and very best anthologists in the children's book world. Her work includes *Love, Don't Panic: 100 Poems to Save Your Life*, *Wizard Poems*, *Best Friends* and *Christmas Poems*. Her unparalleled knowledge of poetry and children's books has come about, in part, through Fiona's previous incarnations as a bookseller, publisher, reviewer, author and in her current position as Editorial Director of Troubadour, the highly successful school-book-fair company.

Fiona lives in Dorset surrounded by thousands of books and some very discerning cats.

Red Lorry, Yellow Lorry

Poems about cars, trains, trucks
and other things that go

chosen by

Fiona Waters

Illustrated by Jane Eccles

MACMILLAN CHILDREN'S BOOKS

For Ryan, with much love from GAF

Associated companies throughout the world

ISBN: 978-0-330-44338-8

1 3 5 7 9 8 6 4 2

A CIP catalogue record for this book is available from
the British Library.

Typeset by Tony Fleetwood
Printed and bound in Great Britain by Mackays of Chatham plc, Kent

Contents

How to Get from A-Z

Ark,
Balloon,
Cruise,
Dodgem car,

Escalator – going far?
Ferry,
Glider,
Heliport,
Intercity,
Juggernaut.

Kart,
Lift,
Moped,
Narrowboat,
Oars,

Pram,
Quad bike,
Raft afloat!
Skateboard,
Taxi,
Underground,

Van,
Walk,
eXpress train,
Yacht. Found
Zeppelin to end my list.
(Bet you've thought of some
I've missed!)

Sue Cowling

motorway

beneath me
where I stand on the bridge
like the captain
of an ocean-going liner

w
a   s
v   e
e   o   a
                       f
u   s
p   t   o
o   r   u
n   a   n
                       f   d
w   f
a   i
v   c
e

coaches, caravans, lorries, cars,
container wagons, land rovers,

l
i
n
e

o
n

l
i
n
e

o
n

l
i
n
e

r
o
w

o
n

r
o
w

o
n

r
o
w

g
o

l
i
k
e

t
h
e

t
i
d
e

never ending,
never ending.

Joan Poulson

Traffic

Wagons snap like dragons
bumping down the road,
trucks are rumbling dinosaurs
with a heavy load,
cars pass with a whispered hiss,
motorcycles growl,
buses scream as shifted gears
change down from yowl to howl.

Listen to the traffic.
Hear its savage sounds.
Fear the mumble-jumble
in the
jungle of
our towns

Gina Douthwaite

Traffic-jam buttie

pavement pavement lamp-post pavement pavement
gutter gutter drain gutter gutter gutter litter drain gutter
car lorry bus car car van truck car fire-engine car tanker
— — — — — — — — — —
bus car car coach minivan car jeep car lorry ambulance
gutter litter gutter drain litter gutter gutter gutter drain
pavement pavement lamp-post pavement pavement

Dave Calder

9

Milk Float

The road is clear
and it's still dark
but someone's made the dogs bark.

Bottles clank.
Now it's in view –
the milk float bringing milk to you.

Jill Townsend

The People Carrier

On our way to school
We all squeeze into
The People Carrier

There's my sister Harriet
My brother Jake
Ed and Aziz
And Benny and Blake
Sarah and Clara
Ali and Dee
Ivor and Ivan
And Rosemary

My mate Billy
His pet worm Clive
And Mum of course
Who has to drive

Now there's no room for me
And it's starting to rain
I'll have to ride up on the roof again

Roger Stevens

Blue Flashing Light

On the top of an ambulance
A blue flashing light
Travels like a shooting star
Fast through the night.

Here is an emergency,
Somewhere someone's ill,
The blue star is rushing
While the night stands still.

Celia Warren

Cars

Cars curtsy

in procession

along bumpy roads.

Celia Warren

Tube Train

Under the ground
there's a sort of snake
that roars up
out of the night,
with a voice as loud
as an ogre
and eyes that are winking
bright.

It twists and turns
and rattles –
then it stops, and opens wide . . .
and all the tired
travellers come
to sit in the snake's
inside.

Jean Kenward

The Diggers and the Dumpers

The diggers and the dumper trucks
Grew bored one summer night –
They trundled through the city
And they rumbled out of sight . . .

Until they reached the seaside
Where the ocean meets the land!
They HOOTED with excitement
As they scooped the moonlit sand.

They built a mighty castle
With a drawbridge and a shed,
And then they knocked it over
And they dug a hole instead.

At last they all grew thirsty
For some diesel in their tanks –
They roared and rumbled home again
With happy HONKS and CLANKS.

Next morning in the scrapyard
Their puzzled owners found
Seashells on their driving seats
And seaweed on the ground!

Clare Bevan

All Aboard

All aboard the bike!
All aboard the car!
We're going to the seaside.
It isn't very far.

Forget about the bike,
Forget about the car –
All aboard the bus –
There's 35 of us!

Fred Sedgwick

The Bus Ride

It's splendid to sit
on the top of a bus!
You feel like the king of the land;

You can look at all manner
of secret things
and hold the world in your hand . . .

You can pass the school
and the bicycle shop,
and be close to the town-hall clock;

You can see the hospital
chimneys where
the chittering starlings flock,

And all the way
to the end of the street
you can know what the walkers DON'T –

Unless they sit
on top of a bus.
And nearly all of them WON'T!

Jean Kenward

If I Were a Hawk

If I were a hawk I'd circle and stalk,
If I were a toad I'd waddle and walk,
If I were a panther I'd prowl and I'd pace,
If I were a zebra I'd rear and I'd race,
If I were a seagull I'd soar and I'd sail,
If I were a slug I'd trudge and I'd trail,
If I were a snake I'd slide and I'd slither,
If I were a sloth I'd doze and I'd dither,

If I were a hippo I'd trundle and tramp,
If I were a rhino I'd stumble and stamp,
If I were a firefly I'd dart and I'd dance,
If I were a pony I'd plunge and I'd prance,
If I were a swordfish I'd spin and I'd spike –

But as I'm just me
                    I'll ride on my bike.

Clare Bevan

Getting There!

Frogs hop to get around.
Snakes slither on the ground.

And how about fish?
They move their fins
And splish, splash, splish.

And what about worms?
To get around, a worm squirms.

To get around up in the sky,
Birds soar and glide and flap and fly.

Crickets jump while in the grass,
And horses gallop as they pass.

Gazelles can leap real high in the air,
While butterflies flutter everywhere.

Moles and gophers get around
By digging tunnels underground.

Squirrels climb real fast and scurry,
While snails don't seem too much
In a hurry.

But, I find, *I* really like
To get around on my new bike.

Robert Scotellaro

Hump Rump Bump!

We went for a trip on a camel's hump
It cramped our legs and bruised our rumps
As it galloped along with a bump bump bump

We went for a trip with a kangaroo
Sitting in her pouch with a perfect view
And we bounced so high that we almost flew

We went for a trip on an anaconda
It packed its bags and went for a wanda
Zipping through the trees on its jungle Honda

We went for a trip with an albatross
The south winds blew and the great waves tossed
As we made our way to Barbados

We went for a trip on the back of a horse
It was easy to ride
We fell off, of course.

Trevor Millum

Granny on a Moped

My granny has a moped;
She rides it near and far.
It's faster than a bicycle
But slower than a car.

She rides her moped to the shops,
Buys lots of food and then,
Bags dangling from the handlebars,
She rides it home again.

She rides it through the countryside,
She rides it through the town.
She rides it when the weather's fine
And when it's pouring down.

She rides her moped everywhere:
She's ridden it to Spain
And all the way to India
(But got caught in the rain).

She's ridden it to Africa,
Across vast, dusty plains,
Where elephants and rhinos roam
And lions shake their manes.

She's even been to the North Pole
And ridden through the snow.
There's nowhere in the whole wide world
Where Granny will not go.

Next week she's off to China
For a month or maybe two.
She's not going by plane, but by –
Well, you can guess, can't you?

Gillian Floyd

The Caractacus Chariot Company

FOR SALE:
SECOND-HAND WAR CHARIOT

One Careful Owner (rumoured to be
Queen Boudicca of the Iceni)
Low Mileage
Two or Four Horsepower
Wheels with Sharp Knives (if required)
5 months Woad Tax
Blood-Red Bodywork
inlaid with Roman Bones

Has taken part in several
Successful Battles:
    the sacking of Camulodunum
    attacks on Londinium
    many minor skirmishes

Backed by our First Class Druid Warranty

Must be seen to be believed!
Only 3 gold pieces o.n.o.

Will Exchange for quantity
of belts, buckles and bronze shields.

Don't delay, view today, at
THE CARACTACUS CHARIOT COMPANY™

Mike Johnson

The Dragon Wagon

This is the dragon wagon
Coming into town;
The only dragon wagon
Green and gold and brown.
Beware the dragon wagon
Coming down your street;
Beware the dragon wagon
With wheels like fiery feet!

The dragon wagon has twenty doors
Fifty teeth and a hundred claws
Its engine growls and grunts and roars . . .

The dragon wagon has ten headlights
Red flashing for turning right
Shiny wings and a bumper that bites . . .

The dragon wagon has spiky wheels
Its wipers shriek and its tyres squeal:
It's an awful 'orrible automobile!

This is the dragon wagon
Going out of town;
The only dragon wagon
In green and gold and brown.
Remember the dragon wagon
That gave you all a fright
Remember the dragon wagon
Roaring out of sight . . .

Trevor Millum

The Travelling Wardrobe

For Rosemary

Sometimes it stands in a desert –
waves of sand lapping over its feet.
It slips a tweed overcoat, silk lined,
over a dipping dune.

Sometimes it stands on a glacier,
one foot stuck in a crevasse.
The briefest of satin-edged slips
slides from the half-open door.

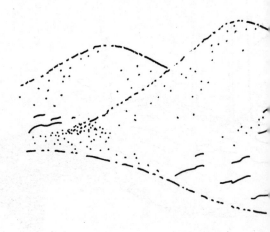

Sometimes it stands on a prairie,
waist high in chafing wheat.
Six pairs of white cotton baby socks
fly in the wind and the heat.

Chrissie Gittins

Rocking Horse

I can
Joust in a tournament,
Ride into battle,
Slay a dragon,
Round up cattle,
Waylay a stagecoach,
Keep crowds at bay
Or just rock dreamily –
Who am I today?

Sue Cowling

On a Narrowboat

We glide along
and watch the view,
then at the lock
there's lots to do.

A narrowboat
is really fun.
Look out! Sit down!
We're in a tunnel!

And now we're out
the other side.
The canal's narrow,
the fields are wide.

So much to see.
But now I'm yawning.
We'll sleep in bunks
until the morning.

Jill Townsend

Tractor

Dressed in a coat of mud
soil with splattered and
the farm tractor coughs and rasps
.throat bad a with horn factory a like

Huge tyres heave
field soggy the through plough the
churning the dark earth into
.waves frozen like shapes
Seagulls swoop and glide behind
free flowing ribbons wild like
in some great wind.

Up and down,
– long day all valley the up and down
the tractor never tires.
pierce lights its evening By
the gathering dusk
fields the over rolls growl its and
like a tumbling echo.
night star-filled the Slowly

covers the countryside in a warm dark

.plough silent own its brings that

John Rice

The lines in this poem do just what a tractor does when it is ploughing a field. First it goes up the field, then it goes down the field. This is an example of 'boustrophedon' or 'ox-writing', where the lines reverse direction but the words do not.

The Train Home

after a day in the city

Backs of grey houses.
Highlights of graffiti.
Warehouses, car parks.
The edge of the city.

A blur of green fields,
Dotted black, brown and white.
Motorways and bridges
Dash past out of sight.

Deep darker than dark,
With a rattle and roar.
A flicker of light.
Then daylight once more.

Rattling through stations,
Can't see what they are.
People can't see us.
We're too fast by far.

A voice saying something
In a musical moan.
Slowing down gently,
We're nearly home.

Pat Gadsby

Walking Joseph

Father, oh father, my shoe's coming off.
I've only to stumble, to spit or to cough
And my lace is undone, my heel out of kilter.
Father, oh father, what shall I do?

You must walk without scuffing or scraping, my son.
You must stride the long road and rejoice, my dear dove.
If you want to get home with the light in the sky,
Son, oh my son, that's what you must do.

Father, oh father, my shoe's full of stones.
They're mighty as rocks. They're breaking my
     bones.
And my legs are all achy. They won't walk any
     further.
Father, oh father, what shall I do?

You must find your best foot and put that foot forward.
You must pull up your socks and tighten your grip.
If you want to get home with the sky clear and bright,
Son, oh my son, that's what you must do.

Father, oh father, you sigh as you walk.
You huff and you puff and wheeze as you talk.
Your back is all bent. You ought to stand straighter.
Father, oh father, what shall we do?

You must get a new father and walk in straight lines.
Your father is old, son. It's past his bed time.
You must stop being curious and heed his advice.
Son, oh my son, that's what you must do.

Brian Morse

Sail Your Silver Boat

The sea is grey, the sky is black
The moon is paper white
Sail your lovely silver boat
Through the silver night
Sail your lovely silver boat
Through the silver night

The sea is green, the sky is blue
Sun shines yellow on the bay
Sail your lovely golden boat
Through the golden day
Sail your lovely golden boat
Through the golden day
  Through the golden day.

Trevor Millum

Bon Voyage: Driving to Paris

Our
dad
never
got
it
right
before
we
left,

so
we
were
on
the

left,

instead
of
right!

Mike Johnson

Inuit Lullaby

Hush now, baby,
Daddy's on a hunting trip,
Gone to catch a fish
And bring it home to you.

Hush now, baby,
Daddy's on a shopping trip,
Gone to the supermarket
On his skidoo!

Sue Cowling

Get On a Toboggan

Hang on
    to the
        toboggan
            And rush
                through the slush
                    and snow

Hang on
    to the
        toboggan
            and
                don't let   go

John Coldwell

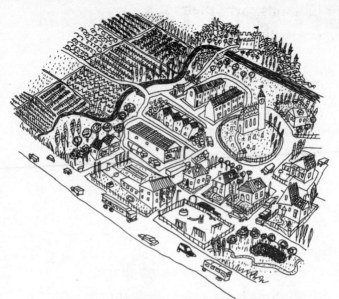

Hot-Air Balloons Floating, Drifting, Turning

Floating
like huge, silent bath bubbles
above the summer greenness.
Drifting
against a red sky
like upturned water droplets.
Turning
gently with the wind's shallow breath
caressing their ribbed skins.

Hot-air balloons carry their
colours across the county.

Some day I'd like to travel in one:
lean out of the basket and
see the ponds below, the fields,
see the woods, the miniature castles.
See the toy-like cars slide along
Kent's straight Roman roads.

Most of all
I'd like to look down on my own village,
my own little house with its little red roof –
and facing the road, my own bedroom window.

If I saw them from above,
and I was floating, drifting, turning,
I'd think of the child
who lives there now and hope
he or she is as happy as I was living there
all those years ago.

Years before I was floating, drifting, turning.

John Rice

The Glider

T   i s
  w   t
         i   g
           n

and t
        u
        r
        n
        i
          n
           g,

Gliding with ease –

    Sp
      i
        n
        n
    ing,
    beginning

to *float* with the breeze;

Lazily,
c r a z i l y
hung
    in the air –

Long way up –
–¡dn ʎɐʍ ƃuoɹʍ
    And never a care!

Trevor Harvey

52

The Lone Ranger

A solitary snowflake
drifts and sways
on its way
past my window,
as it looks for
other snowflakes
that have drifted down before

Then, without a sound,
it touches the ground

and, like them, disappears

as another snowflake
in its wake
starts on the same downward
journey

and with the same result

Trevor Harvey

Armchair Travel

When I was a child
I roamed the world
Safe in my mum's armchair.
I rode wild horses
Over hot desert sands,
Brave and free from care.
I sailed huge ships across stormy seas;
Flew planes over snow-white lands.
I drove buses and trams
With skilful ease,
Their passengers safe in my hands.
The armchair was my motorbike,
My stagecoach, train, my car.
At the click of a switch inside my head,
I travelled near or far.

And all the while I was travelling
And dreaming some magical dream,
My mum washed clothes
At the kitchen sink,
The kitchen wreathed in steam.

Now I am old and grey and tired,
But I sit in Mum's armchair still.
I dream of my childhood travelling.
I hope that I always will.

John Kitching

Cardboard Box Adventure

A cardboard box! We climb inside.
There's never been a better ride.
My sister sits right next to me;
We go down deep below the sea.
We see a giant octopus!
His head is bigger than a bus!
His arms are wiggling everywhere.
We quickly zip away from there.
We steer towards deepest outer space.
Land on a planet – what a place!
We hear an eerie spooky sound.
Then creatures pop up from the ground.
They all have horns and purple hair.
We quickly zoom right out of there!
We race through lots of shooting stars –
Escape some rocket ships from Mars.
We land back home – we climb outside.
There's never been a better ride.

Robert Scotellaro

Porkoplane

When I go flying on my pig
up high into the air,
the people shout,
'How huge! How stout!
How did it get up there?'

I sit behind its flapping ears
and grunt a cheerful tune
as we hunt for
acorns in the clouds or
truffles on the moon.

Back home we eat baked cheesy beans
from buckets on the floor
then end the day
curled up in hay
and snore and snore and snore.

Dave Calder

Icarus

Icarus thought that he could fly
Like a seagull in the sky.
He made some wings with wood and tacks,
And stuck the lot with sealing wax.
Then, climbing to a cliff-top high
He launched himself into the sky.

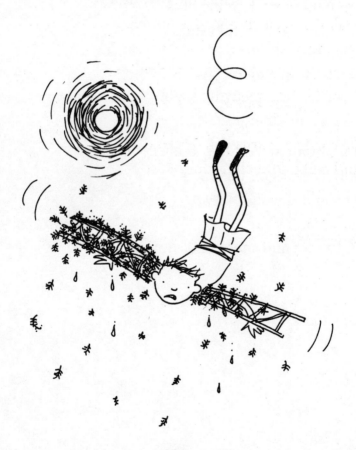

He soared and swooped without a care,
He flapped and fluttered through the air.
Then, on a current he was lifted
And upwards through the clouds he drifted.
He did not think it such good fun
When Icarus felt the fiery sun.
Its burning rays shone on his back,
And melted all the sealing wax.
You should have heard the dreadful yell,
As down to earth poor Icarus fell.
The moral of this tale is clear:
Make sure you have the proper gear
If you go flying way up high,
Like a seagull in the sky,
Or you like Icarus will descend
And come to such a sticky end.

Gervase Phinn

Space Poem

This space
That space
Its space
My space
Who's space
Our space
Their space
Yours

His space
Her space
No space
Some space
What space
This space
That space
There.

Patricia P. Jones

Moonshot

(A Rubai)

I fix my eyes upon the Moon.
They launched my ship at noon.
I'm speeding fast through day and night.
I'll make my landing soon.

John Kitching

*The rubai (plural: rubaiyat) is a Persian verse form. Each rubai
stanza is a quatrain, in which lines 1, 2 and 4 all rhyme.*

Space Traveller

Why did a dog
(or was it a monkey?)
have to be the first animal
to go up into space?
Why did a dog get picked
and not our cat
or Tom Tom the Piper's son's pig?
Why couldn't it have been Sandy
    the Blackpool beach donkey
    a hippopotamus
    or something more interesting than
    a dog?
Actually, I think it should have been
    a tortoise.
It would have been really nice
    for a tortoise
    to get somewhere
    before anyone else.

Peter Dixon

Going Up in the World!

When I grow up I'm going to be
the first postman in *SPACE*!
I'll take the mail to aliens
in every far-off place.
I'll have my very own rocket ship
to zoom about the stars
on trans-galactic postal trips
from Jupiter to Mars.

I'll set off very early
as I jet off on my round;
I'll travel fast! I'll have a blast! –
my feet won't touch the ground!
Delivering my messages
at supersonic speed –
imagine all the languages
I'll have to learn to read!

A letter from a Martian
to a pen pal on the moon;
an invite from the planet Zong
to come and visit soon!
Yes, it's a job in space for *me* –
it's what I dream of most;
as soon as there's a vacancy . . .
I'm taking up the post!

Graham Denton

The Space Ark

Old Noah built a spaceship,
A shiny metal ark,
And when the rains came pouring down
He dived into the dark.

He sailed across the universe
With creatures two by two,
Delighted to be captain of
A supersonic zoo.

The elephants and hippos
Were given king-sized suits,
The woodlice and the centipedes
Wore lots of silver boots.

The tiger found a sleeping bag
With stripes to match his coat.
The pythons and the tortoises
Discovered they could float.

The glow-worms counted comet tails
For forty fiery nights,
The moles felt rather dizzy as
They weren't too keen on heights.

The parrots squawked a message
For the aliens to find,
The sloths just kept on snoring, but
Old Noah didn't mind.

And when the floods were over
He brought them home one day.
(They all felt slightly space-sick
But no one liked to say.)

And now, when skies are cloudy
And storm winds start to blow,
The animals still dream about
Their space ride long ago.

Clare Bevan

The Man, the Moon and the Microlight

High up high
on his way to who cares where,
a goggled man aboard an insect.
Paper-white wings against a darkening sky,
high up high.

High up high
on his way to who says where,
a marching moon in a middle time.
Silver paper circle against a darkening sky,
high up high.

John Rice

Come Fly with Me

My rocket's big enough for two,
Come climb on board with me,
We'll set the engines roaring
With this electronic key,
Boot up the inboard computer,
Then settle down to tea.

I know the risks we're taking,
But we will be all right:
We won't get burnt up by the sun
When it's hot and fiercely bright,
We'll simply delay the blast off
Till the middle of the night.

I really want to check out
If the moon *is* made of cheese
Or if you stand on Pluto
You sink up to your knees
In a sort of gooey seaweed
That also makes you sneeze.

We'll fly the solar system,
We'll orbit Venus and Mars,
We'll wave to all the Little Men
Who make the chocolate bars,
And stock up with a pile of them,
Then whizz off to the stars.

And when we've done a trillion miles
Around the galaxy,
We'll think of heading home again
In triumph, you and me,
Turn on the retro rockets
And land in Battersea!

Matt Simpson

city dragons

late afternoon
and the city
centre
jammed

long-tailed dragons
weave round streets,
fill them, end to end

sounds
of roaring,
snarling
as the beasts
jerk forward,
claim their rights,
engage
in signal-combat
and nose-to-nose
fights.

Joan Poulson

Where Did We Go?

We bought a ticket to . . . Kalamazoo
we went by train
by boat, by plane
around the world
and back again
through night and day
through sun and rain
through mist and snow . . .

Then where did we go?

We bought a ticket to . . . Timbuktu
we went by train
by boat by plane . . .

Then where did we go?

We bought a ticket to . . . Kathmandu
we went by train
by boat by plane . . .

Then where did we go?

77

We bought a ticket to . . . Waterloo
we went by train
by boat by plane . . .

Then where did we go?

We bought a ticket to [you choose some places!]
we went by train
by boat by plane . . .

[last verse]
Then where did we go?
We bought a ticket to . . . Kalamazoo
        to Timbuktu
        to Kathmandu
        to Waterloo
        to [your places!]
we went by train
by boat, by plane
around the world
and back again
through night and day
through sun and rain
through mist and snow . . .

Then where did we go?

Home
sweet
home ! ! !

James Carter

Winter Lights

I fold myself
next to my window
and carefully watch
as the winter darkness
tucks itself slowly around me

Outside,
cars are now giant cats
creeping slowly past
with their great yellow eyes
searching the way home.

In the distance
a train chatters towards me
pulling a necklace of lights
that sparkles along the railway track
until it is sucked into the dark.

Ian Souter

Night Ride

When I can't sleep
I shut my door
And sit on the rug
On my bedroom floor.

I open the window.
I close my eyes
And say magic words
Till my carpet flies:

Zooming over gardens,
Chasing after bats,
Hooting like an owl
And frightening the cats.

Then when I feel sleepy
And dreams are in my head,
I fly back through my window
And snuggle down in bed.

Celia Warren

Driving at Night
with My Dad

Open the window,
the cool summer night swooshes in.
My favourite music playing loud.

2 a.m. – summer's midnight –
neither of us can sleep
so we go for a night drive.

Stars crowd the sky
and twinkle at us in code.
Our headlights reply in light language.

A fox crosses, red and grey,
and arches under a fence;
rabbits run and a farm cat's eyes
catch our beam.
She stares at us for a second of stretched time . . .
. . . her eyes two new coins.

Through villages that are asleep,
past farms that are warm,
past houses that are dreaming,

under trees that are resting,
past birds that have no flight, no song.

I sense I am in some other country,
where day, time, people no longer matter.
In this huge dark,
through the somewhere and the nowhere
of this uninhabited world,
I feel safe and secure
driving at night with my dad.

John Rice

Stairway to the Clouds

I took a stairway to the clouds
And a camel to the moon
A trampoline to Timbuktu
And a rocket to my room

A skateboard to the Red Sea
A submarine to Mars
A freight train to Atlantis
I dived up to the stars

Parachuting on the ocean
I rode my bike down deep
I took a racing car to bed
And drove myself to sleep

I caught a bus that flew
To a bridge across the seas
And then in my canoe
I slalomed through the trees

I scootered on thin ice
Space-hopped into space
With ice skates on the running track
I raced the human race

I bounced upon my pogo stick
All round the equator
I scaled the peak of Everest
Thanks to an elevator

I rope-swung in the city
Piggybacked through town
Rode horses down the rivers
And skied deep underground

I swam across the deserts
And surfed on escalators
I roller-skated on glaciers
And leapfrogged high skyscrapers

I've travelled many places
In many different styles
Near and far and deep and wide
Millions of miles.

But no matter how I wander
No matter where I roam
Of all these special journeys
The best one is . . . back home.

Paul Cookson

A selected list of titles available from
Macmillan Children's Books

The prices shown below are correct at the time of going to press.
However, Macmillan Publishers reserves the right to show new retail prices
on covers, which may differ from those previously advertised.

Fairy Poems	**978-0-330-43352-5**	**£3.99**
Clare Bevan		
Mermaid Poems	**978-0-330-43785-1**	**£3.99**
Clare Bevan		
Space Poems	**978-0-330-44057-8**	**£3.99**
Chosen by Gaby Morgan		

All Pan Macmillan titles can be ordered from our website,
www.panmacmillan.com, or from your local bookshop
and are also available by post from:

Bookpost, PO Box 29, Douglas, Isle of Man IM99 1BQ
Credit cards accepted. For details:
Telephone: 01624 677237
Fax: 01624 670923
Email: bookshop@enterprise.net
www.bookpost.co.uk

Free postage and packing in the United Kingdom